KS2 Maths
Age 10-11

Helen Greaves

Contents

Place value and ordering

See Q1

What does each digit in a whole number show?

Each **digit** in a number has a value which depends on its position. This is called **place value**. Each digit is worth 10 times more than the digit to its right.

Example: 63 794

tens of thousands	thousands	hundreds	tens	units
6	3	7	9	4

See Q2

How do I put whole numbers in the right order?

Numbers can be ordered by comparing the place value of their digits. **Ascending** order means starting with the **smallest** and **descending** order means starting with the **largest**.

Example:
Put these in ascending order
2657, 2567, 2670

2 ⑤ 6 7   2 ⑥ ⑤ 7   2 ⑥ ⑦ 0

Smallest hundreds digit so this number is smallest

Smaller tens digit so this is next smallest

See Q3

What are decimal numbers?

Decimal numbers have digits after the **decimal point**. These represent fractions of units.

Example: 3.71

units	tenths	hundredths
3 •	7	1

See Q4

How do I put decimal numbers in the right order?

As with whole numbers, decimals are ordered by comparing the place value of their digits, including those after the decimal point.

Example:
Put these in ascending order
1.75, 1.77, 1.57

1.⑤7   1.⑦⑤   1.⑦⑦

Smallest tenths digit so smallest number

Smaller hundredths digit so next smallest

Q1

Circle the number whose number 7 digit has a value of 7 thousand.

70089

1708

8917

17204

Q2

For each pair of numbers circle the bigger one.

a) 678   677

b) 5678   5876

c) 19803   19380

Q3

Draw lines to join the numbers whose number 2 digit has the same value.

3.26   12.67   20.6

2.39   23.45   10.2

Q4

Put these numbers in order starting with the smallest.

5.46   6.52   5.49   4.67

Quick Quiz

1   What is the value of the 8 digit in the number 18054? ....

2   Which is smaller: 3489 or 3498? ....

3   What is the value of the 4 digit in the number 3.46? ....

4   What is meant by descending order?
....

5   Which is larger: 5.67 or 5.7? ....

Did You Know?

A billion is a thousand million: 1 000 000 000.

3

Rounding and estimating

See Q1

How can a whole number be rounded?

To round **whole numbers**, look at the digit after the digit to which the number is to be rounded. If it is 4 or less, round down. If it is 5 or more, round up.

Examples: Round the number 7354

stays as 5 as next digit is only 4

7 3 5 ④ To nearest ten   7 3 5 0

goes up to 4 as next digit is 5

7 3 ⑤ 4   To nearest hundred   7 4 0 0

See Q2

How can a decimal number be rounded?

As well as rounding to the nearest ten, hundred and thousand, **decimal numbers** can also be rounded to the nearest unit or whole number.

Example: Round 12.8 to the nearest whole number

goes up to 3 as next digit is 8

1 2 . ⑧   1 3

See Q3

Is there another way to round decimal numbers?

Sometimes numbers with lots of digits after the decimal point are rounded to **1 decimal place**, or the nearest tenth.

Example: Round 8.73 to 1 decimal place

stays as 7 as next digit is only 3

8 . 7 ③   8 . 7

See Q4

How can I estimate answers to calculations?

You can use **rounded numbers** to **estimate** answers to calculations.

Example: Estimate the answer to 13.77 + 9.38

Round 13.77 to 14 and 9.38 to 9 then do 14 + 9 to give 23. The actual answer is 22.95.

Q1

a) What is 2140 rounded to the nearest thousand?

Circle the correct answer.

1000   2000   3000

b) What is 5682 rounded to the nearest hundred?

Circle the correct answer.

5700   5600   5680

Q2

Round each of these decimal numbers to the nearest whole number.

a) 4.57

b) 12.31

c) 10.7

Q3

Each of these numbers has been rounded to one decimal place. Match each number to its rounded one by drawing lines to join them.

4.67   4.6

4.52   4.7

4.58   4.5

Q4

An MP3 player costs £35.69 and a set of earphones costs £8.25. By rounding the prices to the nearest £, estimate the total cost of the MP3 player and earphones.

Quick Quiz

1 What is 452 rounded to the nearest ten?
   ....

2 What is 678 rounded to the nearest hundred? ....

3 What is 6935 rounded to the nearest thousand? ....

4 What is 34.6 rounded to the nearest whole number? ....

5 What is 2.62 rounded to one decimal place? ....

Did YOU Know?

In everyday life, rounding to the nearest thousand is often used for attendances at football matches, for prices of houses and people's salaries.

Special numbers

See Q1

What is the difference between odd and even numbers?

Even numbers end in 0, 2, 4, 6 or 8. All even numbers can be divided exactly by 2.
Odd numbers end in 1, 3, 5, 7 or 9.

See Q2

What is the difference between factors and multiples of a number?

Factors are numbers that divide **exactly** into a number.

Example: Factors of 10 are 1, 2, 5 and 10

A good way to find the factors of a number is to think of the pairs of numbers which multiply to give that number: 1 x 10 and 2 x 5.

Multiples of a number can be thought of as the answers to its **times table**.

Example: Multiples of 10 are 10, 20, 30, 40, 50, ...

See Q3

What is a prime number?

A **prime number** only has two factors: 1 and the number itself.

Example: 13 only has factors of 1 and 13 so it is a prime number

See Q4

What is a square number?

A **square number** is found by multiplying a number by itself.

Example: 3 squared = 3 x 3 = 9   This can also be written as 3^2.

See Q5

What is a negative number?

When counting **backwards** after zero you continue into **negative numbers**.
Negative numbers can be used for temperatures.

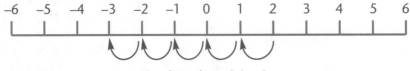

Five less than 2 is −3

Jolly Joke

What did number 98 think about number 3?

He was a little odd!

Q1

Use these digits to make the largest even number possible.

7   2   3   8

Q2

a) Which of these numbers is not a factor of 12?

12   4   8   2

b) Which of these numbers is not a multiple of 12?

12   24   30   120

Q3

Circle the number that is not a prime number.

7   2   15   11

Q4

a) How is a square number found?

....

....

b) What is 2 squared?

....

Q5

a) Which is larger: –8 or –2? ....

b) What is 3 more than –6? ....

Quick Quiz

1   What are odd numbers?

....

2   What are the factors of 8?

....

3   What are the first three multiples of 9?

....

4   What is the value of 4 squared?

....

5   What is a prime number?

....

Did You Know?

2 is the only even prime number.

Number sequences and patterns

See Q1

What is a sequence?

A **sequence** is a **list** of numbers that are **linked** by a **rule**. If you know, or can work out, the rule you can find the next numbers in the sequence.

Examples:

1   4   7   10   13

The numbers go up by three each time, so the rule is add 3. The next number will be 16.

25   23   21   19   17

The numbers go down by two each time, so the rule is subtract 2. The next number will be 15.

See Q2

Can you have negative numbers in a sequence?

Here is an example where some numbers in a sequence are **negative**.

Example: –10   –6   –2   2   6   The rule is add 4

See Q3

Can the rules be more difficult?

In some sequences the next numbers are found by **multiplying** or **dividing**.

Example: 640   320   160   80   40   The rule is divide by 2 (halve)

Some sequences have two rules.

Example: 2   7   17   37   77   The rule is double and add 3

See Q4

Can sequences be shown as patterns?

Some sequences can be drawn as **patterns**.

Example: 3   5   7   9

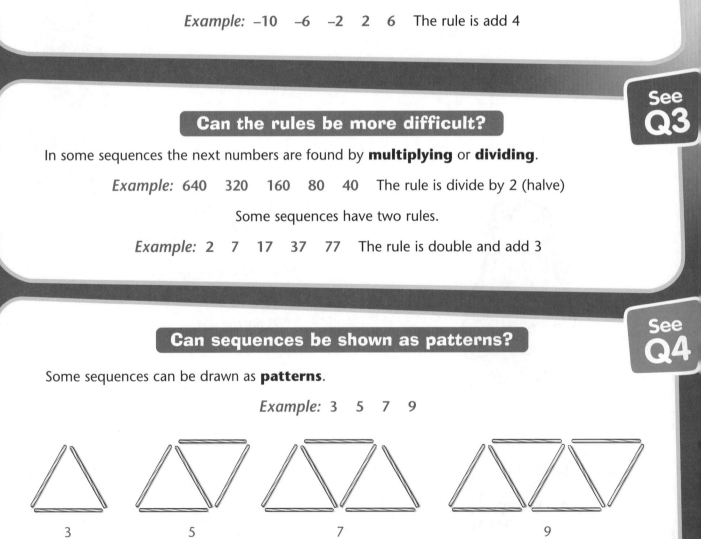

3   5   7   9

Q1

a) What is the rule for this sequence?

3, 8, 13, 18, 23

....

b) What is the next number in this sequence?

35, 31, 27, 23, 19

....

Q2

The rule for this sequence is add on 3.

Find the next two numbers in the sequence.

–13   –10   –7   ....

Q3

Draw lines to match the rule to the correct sequence.

a) 2, 4, 8, 16, 32   double then add 1

b) 1000, 100, 10, 1   multiply by 2

c) 1, 3, 7, 15, 31   divide by 10

d) 1, 3, 9, 27, 81   multiply by 3

Q4

Draw the next pattern in the sequence. Write down the number of matchsticks needed to make it.

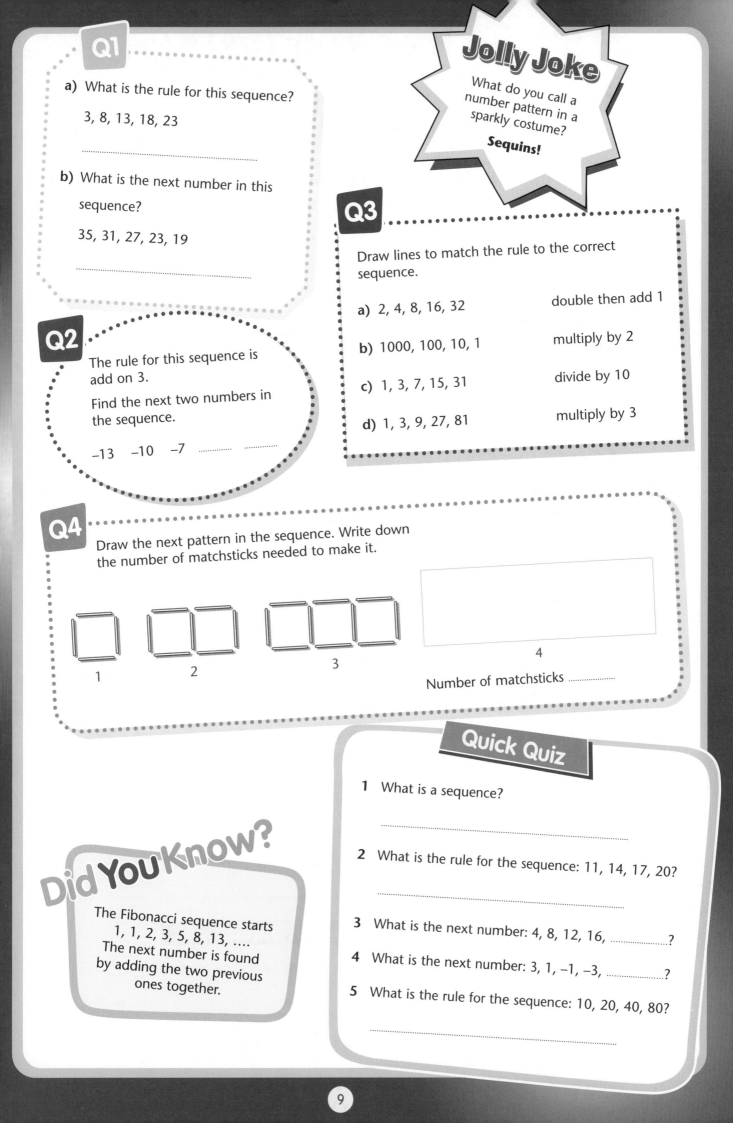

1   2   3   4

Number of matchsticks ....

Quick Quiz

1   What is a sequence?

....

2   What is the rule for the sequence: 11, 14, 17, 20?

....

3   What is the next number: 4, 8, 12, 16, ...?

4   What is the next number: 3, 1, –1, –3, ...?

5   What is the rule for the sequence: 10, 20, 40, 80?

....

Fractions

See Q1

What is an equivalent fraction?

Equivalent fractions represent the same amount but use different numbers.

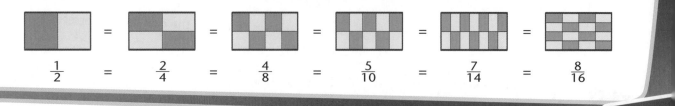

$$\frac{1}{2} \quad = \quad \frac{2}{4} \quad = \quad \frac{4}{8} \quad = \quad \frac{5}{10} \quad = \quad \frac{7}{14} \quad = \quad \frac{8}{16}$$

See Q2

What is a decimal fraction?

A fraction can also be written as a **decimal number**. Here are some you should know:

$$\frac{1}{2} = 0.5 \qquad \frac{1}{4} = 0.25 \qquad \frac{3}{4} = 0.75$$

$$\frac{1}{5} = 0.2 \qquad \frac{1}{10} = 0.1 \qquad \frac{1}{100} = 0.01$$

See Q3

What is meant by 'cancelling' a fraction?

Cancelling, or **simplifying**, a fraction means rewriting the fraction so that it has the smallest possible numbers in the **numerator** (top) and **denominator** (bottom). This is done by dividing top and bottom by the same number.

Example: $\frac{15}{25}$ Divide top and bottom by 5 to get $\frac{3}{5}$

See Q4

Can the numerator in a fraction be bigger than the denominator?

It can! But in this case it is called an **improper fraction**, e.g. $\frac{7}{5}$. An improper fraction can also be written as a **mixed number**. A mixed number is made up of a whole number and a fraction.

Example: $\frac{7}{5} = \frac{5}{5} + \frac{2}{5} = 1 + \frac{2}{5}$ which is written as $1\frac{2}{5}$

Using this idea the other way round:

Example: $1\frac{1}{4} = \frac{4}{4} + \frac{1}{4} = \frac{5}{4}$

See Q5

How do I find a fraction of a quantity?

To find a fraction of a quantity, first divide by the denominator then multiply by the numerator.

Example: Find $\frac{3}{5}$ of 40 kg

First do 40 ÷ 5 to get 8, then x this by 3 to get 24 kg

Q1

All of these fractions, except for one, are equivalent to $\frac{1}{4}$. Which is the odd one out?

$\frac{5}{20}$ $\frac{4}{16}$ $\frac{10}{40}$ $\frac{5}{15}$ $\frac{2}{8}$

Q2

Write the fraction that is equal to each decimal.

a) 0.25

b) 0.01

c) 0.2

Q3

Simplify each fraction giving the answer in its lowest terms (with the smallest numbers possible).

a) $\frac{4}{10}$

b) $\frac{10}{35}$

c) $\frac{9}{12}$

Q4

Circle the correct mixed number that is equal to each improper fraction.

a) $\frac{8}{5}$ = $1\frac{1}{5}$ $1\frac{3}{5}$ $1\frac{3}{8}$

b) $\frac{10}{3}$ = $3\frac{1}{3}$ $1\frac{1}{3}$ $2\frac{2}{3}$

Q5

a) What is $\frac{1}{6}$ of £24?

b) What is $\frac{5}{6}$ of £24?

Did YOU Know?

$\frac{7}{10}$ of the earth is covered by water.

Quick Quiz

1 Complete this equivalent fraction:

$\frac{3}{4} = \frac{?}{12}$ ....

2 What is $\frac{3}{4}$ as a decimal? ....

3 Simplify the fraction $\frac{15}{18}$ ....

4 Write $1\frac{4}{5}$ as an improper fraction.

....

5 What is $\frac{2}{3}$ of 60? ....

Percentages

See Q1

What is a percentage?

A **percentage** means the number of parts in every **hundred**. Fractions of quantities can be written as percentages using the % sign. Here are some useful equivalent fractions and percentages you should know:

$$\frac{1}{2} = 50\% \quad \frac{1}{4} = 25\% \quad \frac{3}{4} = 75\% \quad \frac{1}{10} = 10\% \quad \frac{1}{100} = 1\%$$

See Q2

How do I find the percentage of a shape?

If the shape is divided into 100 equal parts, to shade 7% simply shade in 7 parts. For shapes divided into a different number of parts you need to work out the percentage for each part first.

Example: This shape is divided into 20 equal parts. Each part is 5%.

To show 15% shade 3 parts.

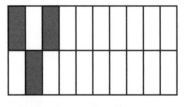

See Q3

How do I find the percentage of a quantity?

For easy numbers you can use mental methods to find a percentage of a quantity.

Example: Find 30% of £50

First find 10% of £50 by dividing by 10 to get £5.

If 10% is £5 then 30% is 3 x £5 = £15

See Q4

How can I use a calculator to find a percentage?

For more difficult percentages you can use a calculator as follows.

Example: Find 23% of 120

On your calculator enter 23 ÷ 100 to get 0.23 then x 120 to get 27.6

Q1

Draw lines to join the fraction to its matching percentage.

$\frac{3}{4}$ 50%

$\frac{1}{10}$ 1%

$\frac{1}{2}$ 10%

$\frac{1}{100}$ 75%

Jolly Joke

Did you know that 8 out of 10 cats prefer Kitty Chunks?

Yes, that's 80 purr-cent!

Q2

Two of these three shapes have the same percentage shaded. Which is the odd one out?

a)   b)   c)

Q3

a) What is 10% of £80?

b) What is 20% of £80?

c) What is 40% of £80?

Q4

Use a calculator to work out these percentages. Tick whether the answer given is correct, or cross if it is wrong.

a) 27% of 300 = 81

b) 65% of 40 = 27

c) 18% of 800 = 144

Quick Quiz

1 What is $\frac{3}{4}$ as a percentage? ....

2 What is 1% as a fraction? ....

3 If a shape is divided into four equal parts and one is shaded, what percentage is this? ....

4 What is 10% of 70 kg? ....

5 What is 20% of £30? ....

Did You Know?

Just over 51% of the UK's population is female and just under 49% is male.

Ratio and proportion

See Q1

What is a ratio?

A **ratio** compares one quantity with another.

Example: There are 3 red and 6 green sweets. There are twice as many green sweets as red. The ratio of red to green sweets is 1 red for every 2 green.

See Q2

What is a proportion?

A **proportion** compares **part** of a quantity with the whole of it. A proportion may be written as a fraction.

Example: There are 8 sweets. 2 are purple and 6 are red. The proportion of purple sweets is 2 out of 8. This can be written as $\frac{2}{8}$ or simplified to $\frac{1}{4}$. That is 1 out of every 4 sweets is purple.

See Q3

How can ratio be used?

When you use a recipe you increase the amounts in the same ratio to make more.

Example:

To make omelettes for 3 people multiply each quantity by 3

2 x 3 = 6 eggs

50 g x 3 = 150 g cheese

Omelette Recipe

Serves 1

2 eggs
50g cheese

How can proportion be used?

See Q4

Finding a proportion is a bit like working out a **fraction of a quantity**.

Example:

There are 30 children in Class 6. The proportion of boys is $\frac{1}{3}$. This means that 1 out of every 3 children is a boy, so 10 out of 30 must be boys.

Jolly Joke

Did you know that 5 out of every 4 people have a problem with proportion?!

Q1

Here is a box of shapes. Tick the statement that is true about the ratio of circles to squares.

a) There is 1 circle for every 3 squares. ☐

b) There is 1 circle for every 4 squares. ☐

c) There is 1 square for every 4 circles. ☐

Q2

Here are some boxes of shapes. In which box is the proportion of stars $\frac{1}{3}$?

a)

b)

c)

☐

Q3

This recipe makes 1 sandwich cake. Write the ingredients needed to make 4 sandwich cakes.

Recipe

100 g flour
100 g butter
100 g sugar
2 eggs

.... g flour

.... g butter

.... g sugar

.... eggs

Q4

A class has 24 children in it. The proportion of girls is $\frac{1}{4}$. How many girls are there in the class?

☐

Did You Know?

The proportion of fat in crisps is $\frac{1}{3}$.

Crisps

Quick Quiz

1 A ratio compares one quantity with the whole of it. True or false? ....

2 How can a proportion be written? ....

3 A bag contains 5 red and 5 black sweets. Write this as a ratio. ....

4 A bag contains 2 green and 4 yellow sweets. What proportion of the sweets are green? ....

5 For the sweets in the question above, what proportion of the sweets are yellow? ....

Addition and subtraction

How can I add numbers mentally?

See Q1

This very much depends on the numbers you are working with. There are lots of different ways.

Example: Add 35 and 37

Either double 35 to get 70 then add the extra 2 from the 37 to get 72
Or add 30 and 30 to get 60, then add 5 and 7 to get 12, now add 60 and 12 to get 72

How can I subtract numbers mentally?

See Q2

The method you use depends on the numbers.

Example: Subtract 18 from 49

Either round 49 to 50, do 50 take away 18 to get 32, then take off 1 as 50 is 1 more than 49 to get the answer 31 **Or** count on from 18 to 49

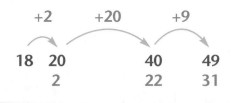

How can I add larger numbers?

There are different ways to do this but a written column method is one possible way.

Example: Add 2359 and 712

See Q3

$$\begin{array}{r} 2\ 3\ 5\ 9 \\ 7\ {}_1 1\ 2\ + \\ \hline {}_1 3\ 0\ 7\ 1 \end{array}$$

How can I subtract larger numbers?

There are various ways but the written column method is a good one to use.

Example: Subtract 187 from 375

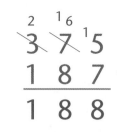

See Q4

How can I add and subtract decimal numbers?

See Q5

Easy decimal number calculations, such as 0.3 + 0.5, can be done mentally. For more difficult numbers, including money calculations, use a written column method – just remember to line up the decimal points.

Example: 1.63 – 0.9

line up decimal points

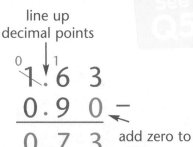

add zero to fill in gap

Draw lines to join the correct answer to its question. Do these mentally.

43 + 47   100

67 + 18   90

39 + 61   82

23 + 32 + 27   85

Jolly Joke

Who was the first maths student?

Add 'em!

Q2

Tick whether the answer is correct, cross if it's not. Do these mentally.

a) 76 − 25 = 51 ☐

b) 54 − 38 = 24 ☐

c) 88 − 49 = 41 ☐

Q3

Work out each calculation using a written method.

a) 378 + 649

b) 1970 + 2451

Q4

Work out each calculation using a written method.

a) 843 − 227

b) 2569 − 1374

Work out each calculation using a written method.

a) 8.67 + 3.4

b) 7.82 − 3.14

Quick Quiz

1 What is 18 + 32? ....

2 What is 59 + 33? ....

3 What is 126 − 72? ....

4 What is 32 + 25 − 18? ....

5 What is 0.26 + 0.36? ....

Did You Know?

The + symbol, meaning add, is thought to have been first used in the fourteenth century.

Multiplication and division

See **Q1**

How can I multiply numbers mentally?

It is vital that you know your **times tables**. You can then use these facts to work out harder multiplications in your head using different ways.

Example:

14 x 7   7 x 7 = 49 then double to get 98

23 x 4   20 x 4 = 80 and 3 x 4 = 12, then 80 + 12 = 92

Or double 23 = 46 then double again to get 92

0.6 x 4   6 x 4 = 24, then 'add' decimal point to get 2.4

See **Q2**

How can I divide numbers mentally?

There are different methods but for all of them you need to know your times tables backwards, e.g. 24 ÷ 8 = 3. Remember that some divisions give **remainders**.

Example:

28 ÷ 5   Recall that 25 ÷ 5 = 5 then count on 3 to 28 to give the answer 5 remainder 3

96 ÷ 4   Halve 96 to get 48 then halve again to get 24

See **Q3**

How can I multiply larger numbers?

There are a number of ways to do this. Here are two ways:

Example: Multiply 23 by 14

See **Q4**

How can I divide larger numbers?

There are several ways to do this. The method below uses subtraction in 'chunks' to divide.

Example: Divide 170 by 14

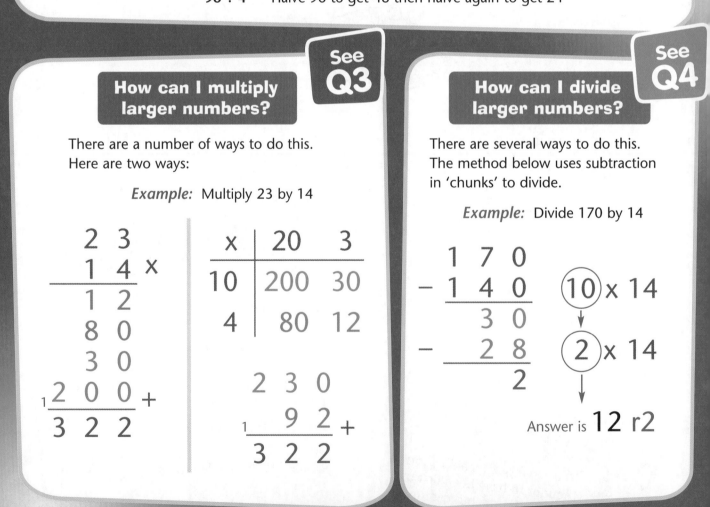

Answer is **12** r2

Q1

Circle all of the multiplications that have the same answer. Work them out mentally.

6 x 8   2 x 24

7 x 9   16 x 3   4 x 13

Q2

All of these divisions have the same answer except for one. Which is the odd one out?

a) 60 ÷ 15   c) 24 ÷ 6

b) 64 ÷ 8   d) 100 ÷ 25

Q3

Use a written method to work out these two multiplications.

a) 256 x 7

b) 24 x 16

Q4

Use a written method to work out these two divisions.

a) 165 ÷ 6

b) 286 ÷ 13

Quick Quiz

1   What is 8 x 8? ....

2   What is 16 x 9? ....

3   What is 63 ÷ 7? ....

4   What is 30 ÷ 4? ....

5   What is 20 x 14? ....

Did You Know?

If you know one multiplication fact you can find 3 other facts. E.g. 5 x 7 = 35 also tells you that 7 x 5 = 35, 35 ÷ 7 = 5 and 35 ÷ 5 = 7.

Problem solving

See **Q1**

What are maths problems?

A problem is a type of question where you need to work out which bits of maths you need to use to get the answer.

Example: A farmer has 4 hens. Each hen lays 9 eggs. How many boxes of 6 can he fill?

| Step 1 | Work out number of eggs | 4 x 9 = 36 eggs (MULTIPLY) |
| Step 2 | Work out number of boxes | 36 ÷ 6 = **6 boxes** (DIVIDE) |

See **Q2**

How do I solve measures problems?

You must make sure that each quantity is in the **same units**. If they aren't, change them first.

Example: A baker uses 300 g flour from a 2 kg bag. How much flour is left?

| Step 1 | Change 2 kg into g | 2 x 1000 = 2000 g |
| Step 2 | Work out how much is left | 2000 – 300 = **1700 g** |

How do I solve time problems?

Many time problems use some sort of timetable, such as TV listings or train times. You need to work out differences between times.

Example: A train leaves York at 1:50 pm and arrives in London at 4:00 pm. How long does it take?

See **Q3**

10 minutes   2 hours

1:50   2:00   4:00   Time taken is 2 hours and 10 minutes

How do I solve money problems?

See **Q4**

As with other problems, decide on the steps you need to take and choose whether to use +, –, x or ÷. Remember to work in either pence or pounds.

Example: A bag of 9 apples costs £1.08. What does each apple cost?

| Step 1 | Change £1.08 into pence | 108p |
| Step 2 | Work out cost of apple | 108 ÷ 9 = **12p** |

If you are using a **calculator** to help you solve a money problem make sure you read the display correctly.

Example: Work out the cost of 15 pencils costing 48p each

Enter this on your calculator as 15 x 0.48 =

The calculator answer is **7.2** but remember to read this as **£7.20**

Q1

Naseem buys 2 packs of 12 cards and 3 packs of 8 cards. How many cards has he bought altogether?

Jolly Joke

What did one maths book say to the other?

Don't bother me, I've got my own problems!

Q2

Kim walks 1.4 km and then runs 700 m. How far has she gone altogether?

a) Give your answer in metres (m).

....

b) Give your answer in kilometres (km).

....

Q3

Here is a TV listing.

6.45	Weakest Link
7.35	National Lottery
8.20	Casualty
9.15	News
9.35	Match of the Day
10.45	Film

a) Circle the programme that lasts 55 minutes.

b) Circle the programme that lasts 1 hour and 10 minutes.

Q4

Fish cost £2.35 each and chips cost 80p a bag.

a) How much would it cost for fish and chips?

b) What change would you get from a £5 note?

c) Use a calculator to work out how much it would cost to buy 6 bags of chips.

Quick Quiz

1 There are 8 cakes in a box. How many cakes in 10 boxes? ....

2 A TV programme starts at 8:20 pm and ends at 10 pm. How long does it last? ....

3 A bag of 7 pears costs £1.05. How much does each pear cost? ....

4 65 cm is cut from a 2 m length of ribbon. How much is left? ....

5 Parking costs 80p an hour. How much does it cost to park for 5 hours? ....

Did You Know?

The decimal money we use today started in 1971. Before that money was given in pounds, shillings and pence.

Probability

See Q1

What is meant by probability?

Probability is a measure of how **likely** it is for something to happen.

Example: It is certain that the day after Friday will be Saturday.

It is impossible that the day after Friday will be Sunday.

There is a good chance that it will snow in December.

See Q2

What is meant by even chance?

In some situations there are only two **outcomes** (things that could happen).
If it is equally likely that each could happen, we say it has an **even chance**.

Example: There is an even chance of a coin landing on either heads or tails

See Q3

How else can I describe probability?

For some events, probability can be given as a **fraction**.
All probabilities are between 0 and 1.

Example:

A coin has 2 faces,
1 of them is heads.
Probability of landing
on heads = $\frac{1}{2}$

Example:

A bag contains 5 balls,
2 of them are blue.
Probability of picking
blue ball = $\frac{2}{5}$

See Q4

Why is a probability scale used?

A **probability scale** can be used to compare the chances of different events.

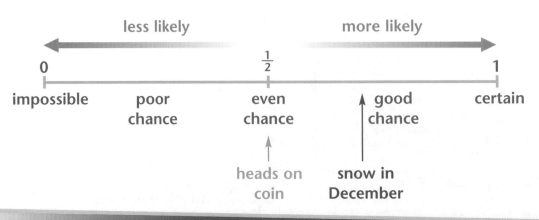

less likely   more likely

0		$\frac{1}{2}$		1
impossible	poor chance	even chance	good chance	certain

heads on coin

snow in December

22

Q1

Tick the statement that is true.

a) There is a good chance it will snow in the desert. ☐

b) It is impossible that Tuesday will be the day after Monday. ☐

c) It is certain that the month before May will be April. ☐

Q2

For which of these spinners is there an even chance of landing on blue? ☐

a)   b)   c)

Q3

Here is a bag of coloured balls.

Circle the correct probability for picking a red ball from the bag.

$\frac{3}{7}$ $\frac{4}{7}$ $\frac{3}{4}$

Q4

Use these words and numbers to complete the probability scale.

even chance   0   certain   good chance   poor chance

....

|————————————————————|
0                    $\frac{1}{2}$ 1

impossible   ....

Quick Quiz

1 What is probability a measure of? ....

2 An even chance happens when there are two equally likely outcomes. True or false? ....

3 Which two values do all probabilities lie between? ....

4 What is the probability of rolling a six on a dice? ....

5 What is the probability of getting tails on a coin? ....

Mode, median, mean and range

See **Q1**

What is the mode?

The **mode** of a set of data is the **most common** item or number.

Example:

A dice is rolled ten times. Here are the scores:

3   4   **3**   6   2   1   **3**   6   5   **3**

The mode, or modal score, is **3**.

See **Q2**

What is the median?

The **median** of a set of data, in order of size, is the **middle** value.

Example:

The heights of five flowers were measured.
Here are the heights in order of size starting with the smallest.

20 cm   25 cm   **27 cm**   30 cm   31 cm

The median height is **27 cm**.

See **Q3**

What is the mean?

The **mean** of a set of data is found by **adding up** all of the values and then **dividing** the total by the number of values.

Example:

Here are five scores in a spelling test:

4   7   10   8   6

Total of scores = 4 + 7 + 10 + 8 + 6 = 35   Mean = 35 ÷ 5 = **7**

See **Q4**

What is the range?

The **range** of a set of data is the **difference** between the largest and smallest numbers.

Example:

In the spelling test above the highest score is 10 and the lowest is 4

Range = 10 – 4 = **6**

Q1

What is the mode of each of these sets of numbers?

a) 3 5 3 7 4 5 3

b) 28 38 27 38 29 35

a) ☐   b) ☐

Q2

Here are the ages of five people:

52   56   39   48   46

a) Write these ages in order, starting with the youngest.

☐

b) Write down the median age. ☐

Q3

Here are the prices of the same CD in four different shops:

£4   £7   £9   £8

What is the mean price of the CD?

☐

Q4

a) How do you find the range of a set of numbers?

....

....

b) Find the range of these test scores:

18   14   8   19   15   ☐

Quick Quiz

1   What is the mode of a set of data? ....

....

2   It doesn't matter if the numbers are not in order when finding the median. True or false? ....

3   What is the mean of 8 and 12? ....

4   Which word is used to describe the number in the middle of an ordered set of numbers? ....

5   What is the mode of 5, 6, 2, 5 and 1? ....

Did You Know?

The average person in the UK spends 18 hours watching TV a week.

Displaying data

See Q1

How can I display sorted numbers?

Here is an example of how to use a Venn diagram. A **Venn diagram** usually has hoops.

odd numbers   multiples of 5

17   **15**   10
31   **35**   40

Here is an example of how to use a Carroll diagram. A **Carroll diagram** is a small table.

	odd	even
multiple of 5	15	40
not a multiple of 5	9	12

See Q2

What is a bar chart?

This is a **bar chart**.

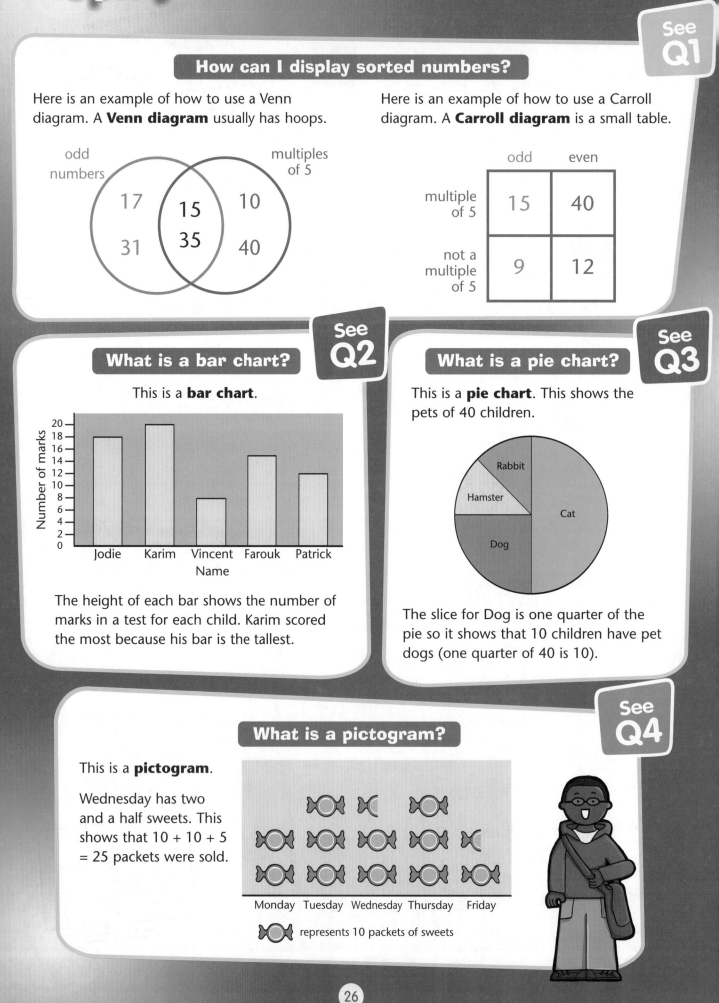

The height of each bar shows the number of marks in a test for each child. Karim scored the most because his bar is the tallest.

See Q3

What is a pie chart?

This is a **pie chart**. This shows the pets of 40 children.

Rabbit
Hamster
Cat
Dog

The slice for Dog is one quarter of the pie so it shows that 10 children have pet dogs (one quarter of 40 is 10).

See Q4

What is a pictogram?

This is a **pictogram**.

Wednesday has two and a half sweets. This shows that 10 + 10 + 5 = 25 packets were sold.

Monday Tuesday Wednesday Thursday Friday

represents 10 packets of sweets

Q1

The diagram shows multiples of 4 and 10.

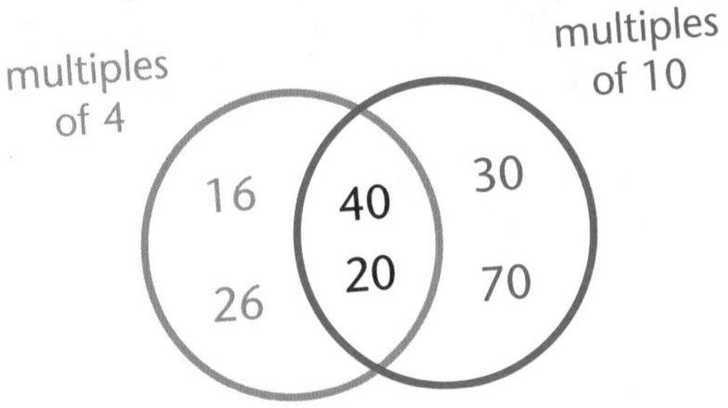
multiples of 4
multiples of 10
16
26
40
20
30
70

a) What type of numbers are displayed in the part of the diagram where the circles cross?

....

b) One of the numbers is wrong. Put a cross through it.

Jolly Joke

What type of animal is used to display data?

A grr-aph!

Q2

The bar chart shows the money raised by five charity events at a school.

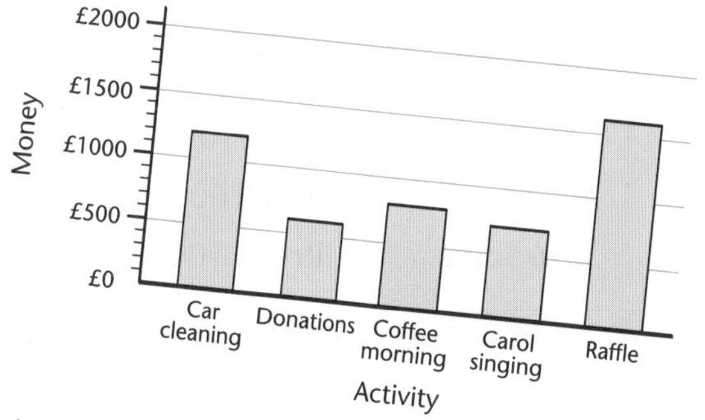
£2000
£1500
£1000
£500
£0
Money
Car cleaning
Donations
Coffee morning
Carol singing
Raffle
Activity

a) Which activity raised the most money?

....

b) How much was raised by carol singing?

....

Q3

The pie chart shows the amount of time spent on different subjects in school each week.

24 hours

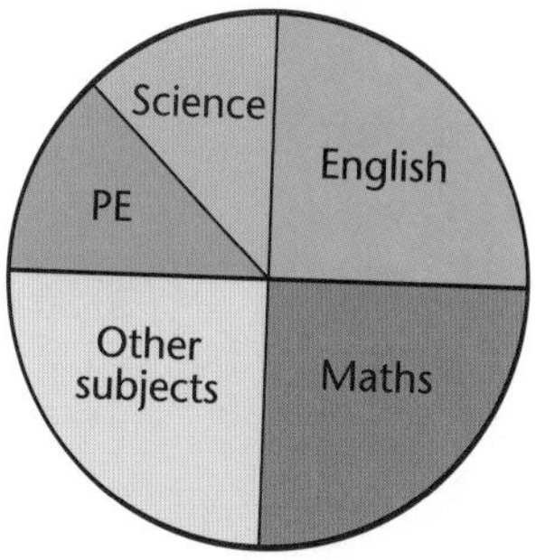
Science
English
PE
Other subjects
Maths

a) How many hours are spent on English?

....

b) How many hours are spent on Science?

....

Q4

The pictogram shows the number of sunny days for four months.

a) How many sunny days were there in August?

....

b) How many sunny days were there in June?

....

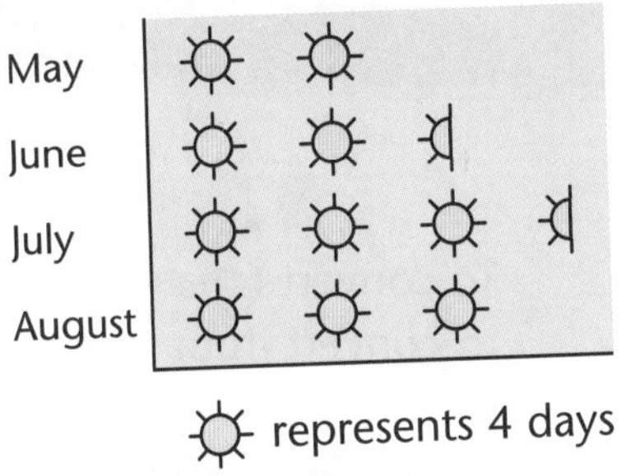
May
June
July
August
represents 4 days

Quick Quiz

1 Which type of diagram is used for sorting numbers in a table? ....

2 What type of chart uses a circle cut into slices?

....

3 What type of chart uses small pictures to show the data? ....

4 Which type of diagram uses overlapping circles?

....

5 Which type of chart uses columns to show the data? ....

Did You Know?

The pie chart was invented just over 200 years ago.

Units and measuring

See Q1

Which units do I need to know?

These are the most commonly used **metric units** and their equivalents.

Length	1 cm = 10 mm; 1 m = 100 cm; 1 m = 1000 mm; 1 km = 1000 m
Mass	1 kg = 1000 g
Capacity	1 litre = 1000 ml

See Q2

Do I need to know any imperial units?

Imperial units are old-fashioned units but they are still used in everyday life so it is useful if you know the most common ones.

Length	8 km is about 5 miles
Mass	1 kg is about 2 pounds
Capacity	1 litre is about 2 pints

See Q3

How do I convert between units?

To convert (change) from 'small' to 'large' units (such as cm to m) **divide**; to convert from 'large' to 'small' units (such as kg to g) **multiply**.

Example: **Write 350 cm as a length in metres**

There are 100 cm in 1 m so work out 350 ÷ 100 to get 3.5 m

Write 5 kg in grams

There are 1000 g in 1 kg so work out 5 x 1000 to get 5000 g

See Q4

How do I read measuring scales?

Measuring equipment often uses scales. Work out how much each division is worth before taking the reading.

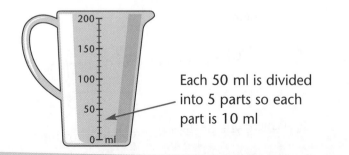

Each 50 ml is divided into 5 parts so each part is 10 ml

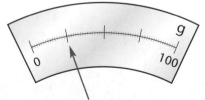

100 g is divided into 4 parts so each part is 25 g

Q1

Complete these equivalent metric units.

a) 100 cm = ...m

b) 1 kg = ... g

c) 1 litre = ... ml

d) 1000 mm = ... cm

Jolly Joke

Who is king of the measuring equipment?

The ruler!

Q2

8 km is about the same distance as 5 miles. How many miles is it to the beach?

Beach 24 km

Q3

Convert each quantity to the units given.

a) 3000 g = ... kg

b) 55 mm = ... cm

c) 4 km = ... m

d) 2.5 l = ... ml

Q4

Here is an apple on some kitchen scales. What is the mass of the apple?

g

0   100   200   300   400

Quick Quiz

1 How many mm are there in 1 cm? ....

2 About how many pounds are there in 1 kg? ....

3 A big carton of milk contains 4 pints. About how many litres is this? ....

4 How many metres are there in 6 km? ....

5 How many litres is 2400 ml? ....

Did You Know?

There are 1 million millimetres in a kilometre.

Perimeter and area

See **Q1**

What is the perimeter of a shape?

The **perimeter** of a shape is the **distance around** the outside. It is measured in length units such as centimetres (cm) or metres (m).

Add together the lengths of the sides

Perimeter $= 10+9+7$ cm
$= 26$ cm

See **Q2**

How can I find the perimeter of a shape on a grid?

If the shape is drawn on a centimetre squared grid you can work out the perimeter by **counting** the number of 1 centimetre lengths around the outside.

perimeter 8 cm   perimeter 10 cm

See **Q3**

What is the area of a shape?

The **area** of a shape is the amount of **space** it covers. It is measured in square units such as cm² or m². If the shape is drawn on a centimetre squared grid the area can be found by counting squares.

1	2	3
4	5	6

Area 6 cm²

1	2	3

Area 4 cm²

two half squares make 1 whole square

See **Q4**

How can I work out the area of a rectangle?

If you know the **length** and the **breadth** of the rectangle, you can work out the area.

3 cm

5 cm

Area $= 5$ cm $\times 3$ cm
$= 15$ cm²

Area = length x breadth

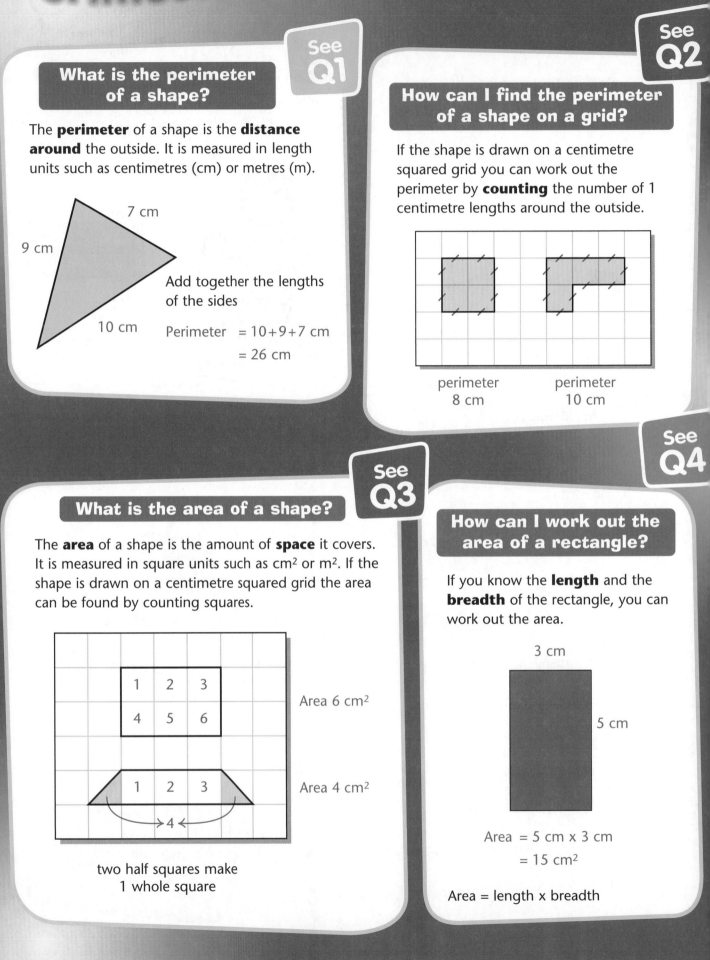

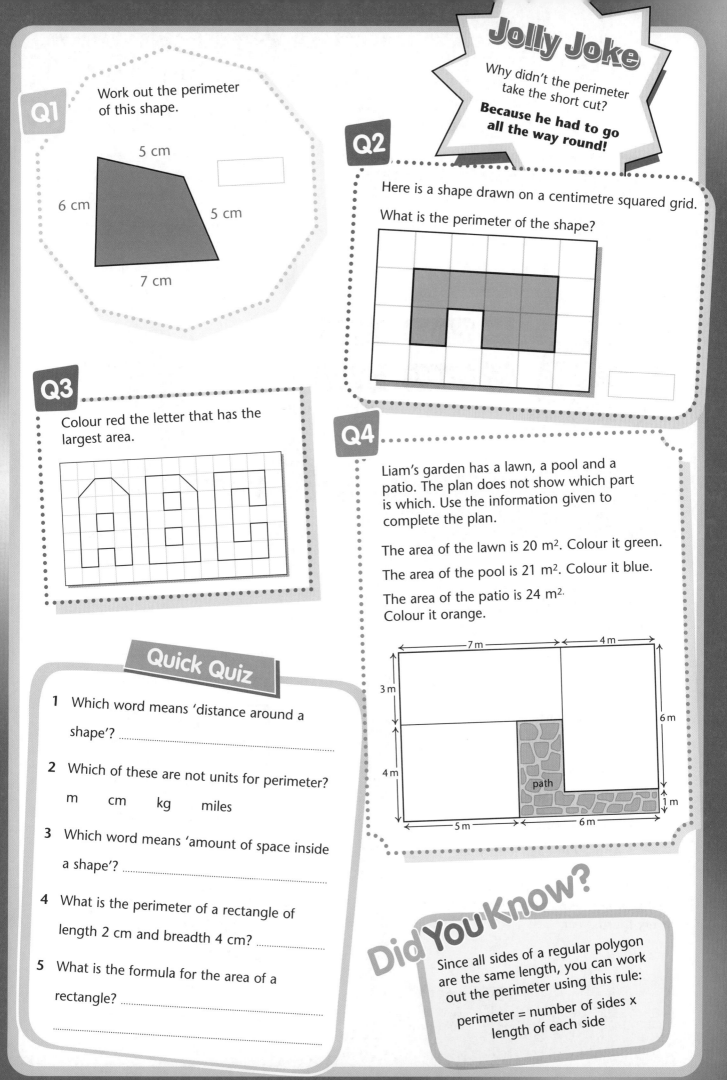

Q1 Work out the perimeter of this shape.

5 cm

6 cm   5 cm

7 cm

Jolly Joke

Why didn't the perimeter take the short cut?

Because he had to go all the way round!

Q2

Here is a shape drawn on a centimetre squared grid.

What is the perimeter of the shape?

Q3

Colour red the letter that has the largest area.

Q4

Liam's garden has a lawn, a pool and a patio. The plan does not show which part is which. Use the information given to complete the plan.

The area of the lawn is 20 m². Colour it green.

The area of the pool is 21 m². Colour it blue.

The area of the patio is 24 m². Colour it orange.

7 m   4 m

3 m

6 m

4 m

path

5 m   6 m   1 m

Quick Quiz

1 Which word means 'distance around a shape'? ....

2 Which of these are not units for perimeter?
   m   cm   kg   miles

3 Which word means 'amount of space inside a shape'? ....

4 What is the perimeter of a rectangle of length 2 cm and breadth 4 cm? ....

5 What is the formula for the area of a rectangle? ....
   ....

Did You Know?

Since all sides of a regular polygon are the same length, you can work out the perimeter using this rule:

perimeter = number of sides × length of each side

Time

See Q1

What are the different ways of showing times?

Clocks can be either **analogue** or **digital**. Digital times can be shown in either 12 hour or 24 hour forms.

ANALOGUE

It's twenty to ten...

DIGITAL

9:40 AM

09:40

9:40 PM

21:40

12 HOUR

24 HOUR

See Q2

What are the different units of time?

1 minute	= 60 seconds
1 hour	= 60 minutes
1 day	= 24 hours
1 week	= 7 days

See Q3

How can I remember how many days there are in each month?

Learn this rhyme to help you remember the number of days in each month:

30 days hath September,

April, June and November.

All the rest have 31,

Except in February alone,

Which has but 28 days clear,

And 29 in each leap year.

Also remember that there are 365 days in a year and 366 in a leap year – that's every fourth year.

See Q4

How can I convert between units of time?

To change from minutes to seconds x **by 60**

To change from hours to minutes x **by 60**

To change from seconds to minutes ÷ **by 60**

To change from minutes to hours ÷ **by 60**

Running Time:

120 mins

DVD

120 ÷ 60 = 2 hours

3ᴍ25ꜱ

3 x 60 = 180 seconds then
180 + 25 = 205 seconds

Q1

Colour the clocks showing the same time with the same colour.

Q2

Complete these sentences.

a) There are .... hours in 1 day.

b) There are .... minutes in 1 hour.

Q3

Here are the pages for June and July from a calendar.

JUNE

Sun	Mon	Tue	Wed	Thu	Fri	Sat
		1	2	3	4	5
6	7	8	9	10	11	12
13	14	15	16	17	18	19
20	21	22	23	24	25	26
27	28	29	30			

JULY

Sun	Mon	Tue	Wed	Thu	Fri	Sat
				1	2	3
4	5	6	7	8	9	10
11	12	13	14	15	16	17
18	19	20	21	22	23	24
25	26	27	28	29	30	31

- James' birthday is on 18th June. Mark this on the calendar with a star *.

- James goes on holiday on the 27th June for 10 days. Mark the day he comes back on the calendar with a cross X.

- James' brother's birthday is on the third Wednesday in July. Circle this date on the calendar.

Q4

Milly took 250 minutes to run a marathon. How long was this in hours and minutes?

Quick Quiz

1 How many days are in June? ....

2 How many minutes are in 2 hours?
   ....

3 How many days are in 3 weeks?
   ....

4 How many minutes is 180 seconds?
   ....

5 How would you write 2:30 pm as a 24 hour clock time? ....

2D shapes: triangles, quadrilaterals and polygons

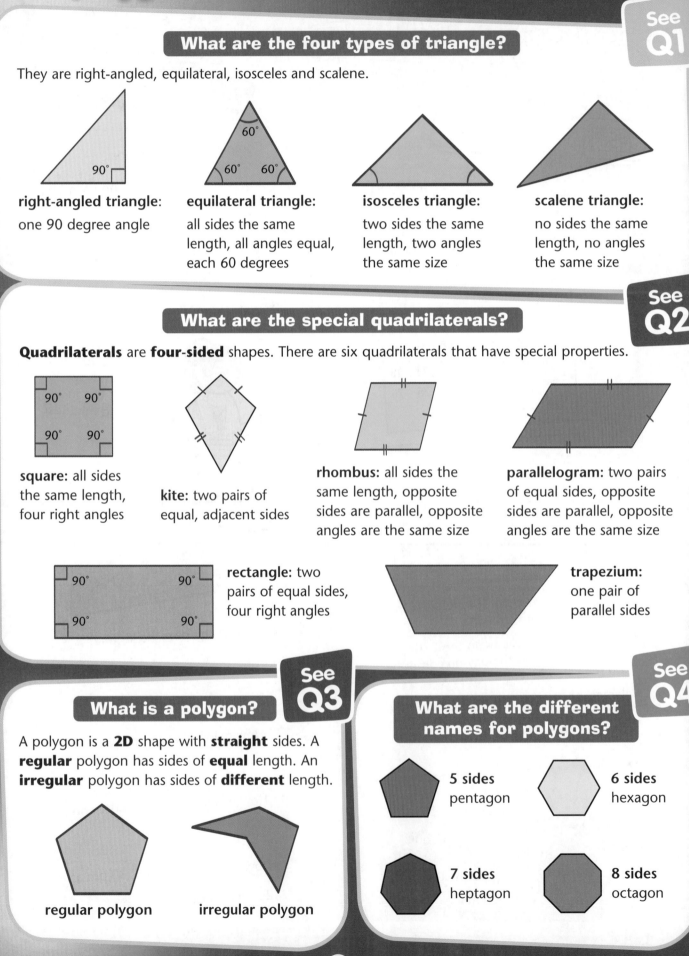

See Q1

What are the four types of triangle?

They are right-angled, equilateral, isosceles and scalene.

right-angled triangle: one 90 degree angle

equilateral triangle: all sides the same length, all angles equal, each 60 degrees

isosceles triangle: two sides the same length, two angles the same size

scalene triangle: no sides the same length, no angles the same size

See Q2

What are the special quadrilaterals?

Quadrilaterals are **four-sided** shapes. There are six quadrilaterals that have special properties.

square: all sides the same length, four right angles

kite: two pairs of equal, adjacent sides

rhombus: all sides the same length, opposite sides are parallel, opposite angles are the same size

parallelogram: two pairs of equal sides, opposite sides are parallel, opposite angles are the same size

rectangle: two pairs of equal sides, four right angles

trapezium: one pair of parallel sides

See Q3

What is a polygon?

A polygon is a **2D** shape with **straight** sides. A **regular** polygon has sides of **equal** length. An **irregular** polygon has sides of **different** length.

regular polygon   irregular polygon

See Q4

What are the different names for polygons?

5 sides
pentagon

6 sides
hexagon

7 sides
heptagon

8 sides
octagon

Q1

Tick the statements that are true.

a) A scalene triangle has no sides of the same length. ☐

b) An isosceles triangle has three equal angles. ☐

c) An equilateral triangle has three sides of equal length. ☐

Jolly Joke

What did the mathematician say when he found that his parrot had disappeared?

Where's my poly-gon?!

Q2

For each quadrilateral put a tick if the shape has that property and a cross if it doesn't.

shape	4 equal sides	4 right angles
rectangle	✗	✓
square		
parallelogram		
rhombus		

Q3

Is this statement true or false?

An irregular polygon has sides that are all the same length.

....

Q4

Name these polygons.

a)

....

b)

....

Quick Quiz

1 What type of triangle has two sides of equal length? ....

2 What is special about a right-angled triangle? ....

3 Which shape has just one pair of parallel sides? ....

4 Which two shapes have four right angles? ....

5 What is the name of a six-sided polygon? ....

Did You Know?

20p and 50p coins are heptagons – they have 7 sides.

2D shapes: symmetry

See Q1

What is reflective symmetry?

If a line can be drawn through a 2D shape so that the shape on either side of the line looks exactly the same, it is called a **line of symmetry**. The shape is said to have **reflective symmetry**.

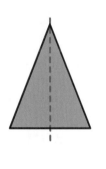

See Q2

Can a 2D shape have more than one line of symmetry?

Some shapes do have 2 or more lines of symmetry.

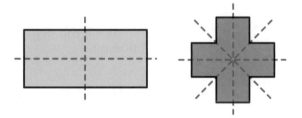

A **regular polygon** has as many lines of symmetry as it has sides.

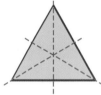 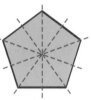

equilateral triangle   regular pentagon   regular octagon

See Q3

Can a 2D shape have no lines of symmetry?

Yes it can! If a shape has no lines of symmetry, it is said to not have reflective symmetry.

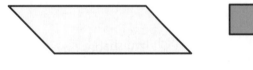

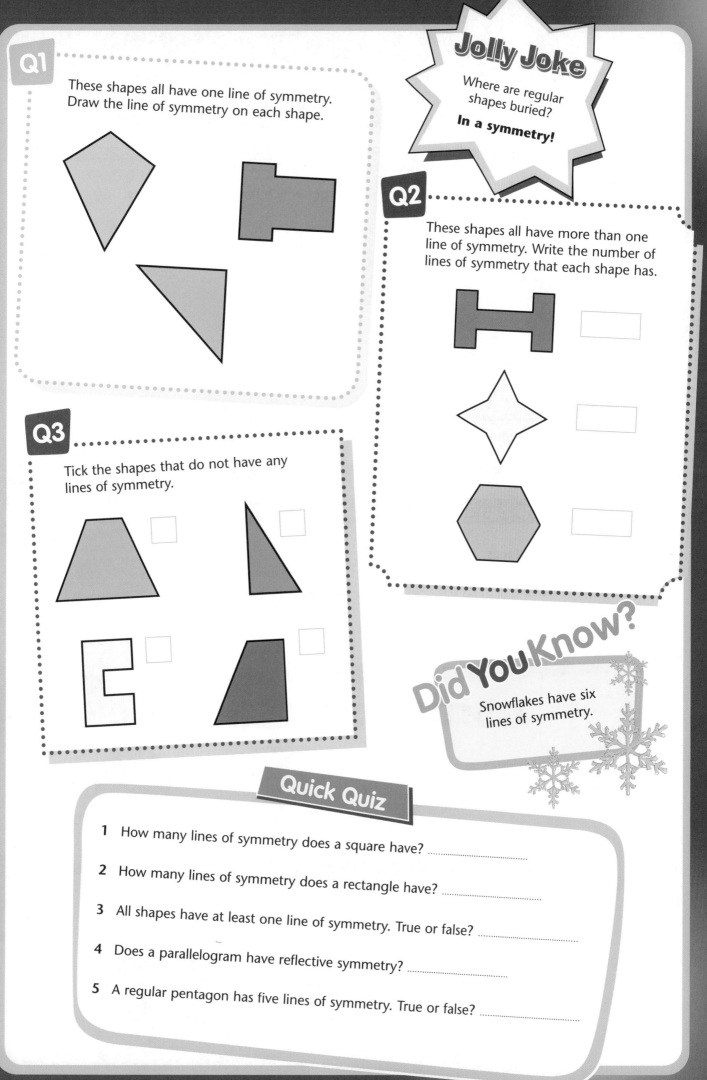

Q1

These shapes all have one line of symmetry. Draw the line of symmetry on each shape.

Q2

These shapes all have more than one line of symmetry. Write the number of lines of symmetry that each shape has.

Q3

Tick the shapes that do not have any lines of symmetry.

Did You Know?

Snowflakes have six lines of symmetry.

Quick Quiz

1 How many lines of symmetry does a square have? ....

2 How many lines of symmetry does a rectangle have? ....

3 All shapes have at least one line of symmetry. True or false? ....

4 Does a parallelogram have reflective symmetry? ....

5 A regular pentagon has five lines of symmetry. True or false? ....

3D shapes

See Q1

Which 3D shapes should I know?

You should be able to recognise the following shapes which have only **flat faces**.

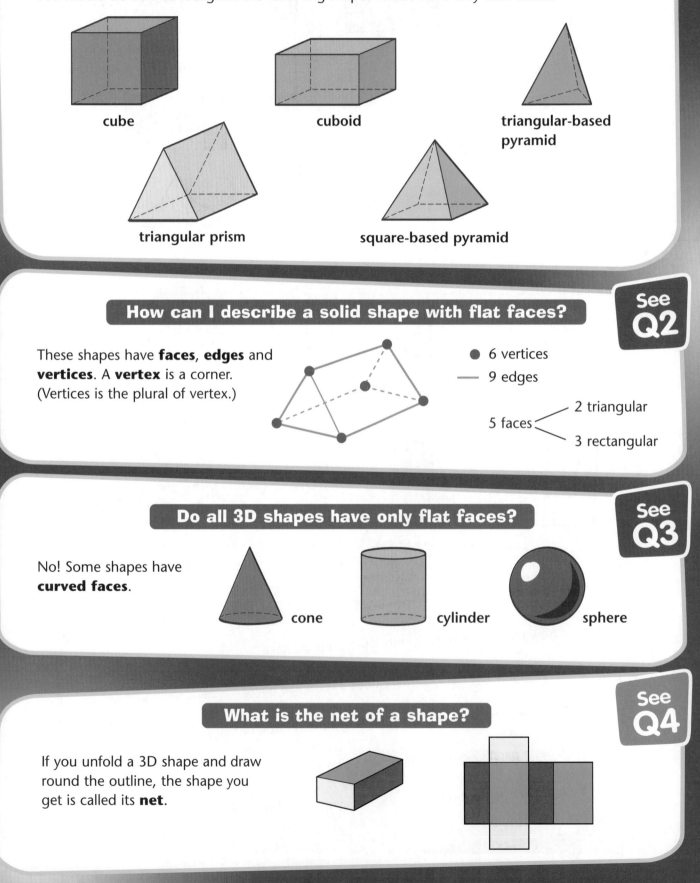

cube

cuboid

triangular-based pyramid

triangular prism

square-based pyramid

See Q2

How can I describe a solid shape with flat faces?

These shapes have **faces**, **edges** and **vertices**. A **vertex** is a corner. (Vertices is the plural of vertex.)

● 6 vertices

— 9 edges

5 faces ⟨ 2 triangular
         3 rectangular

See Q3

Do all 3D shapes have only flat faces?

No! Some shapes have **curved faces**.

cone   cylinder   sphere

See Q4

What is the net of a shape?

If you unfold a 3D shape and draw round the outline, the shape you get is called its **net**.

Q1

Draw lines to join each shape to its name.

square-based pyramid

triangular-based pyramid

triangular prism

Q2

Complete the number of faces, edges and vertices for these two shapes. Two have been done for you.

.... faces

.... vertices

12 edges

4 faces

.... vertices

.... edges

Q3

a) Which shape has two circular faces and one curved face?

....

b) Which shape has no flat faces?

....

Q4

Here is a net of a 3D shape. Circle the name of the shape.

triangular prism   cylinder

square-based pyramid   cube

Quick Quiz

1   What shape is a dice? ....

2   What is the mathematical name for the corner of a 3D shape? ....

3   What shape are the faces of a cube? ....

4   What is the mathematical name for a ball? ....

5   Which name is given to a 'flattened-out' 3D shape?

....

Did You Know?

The famous Great Pyramid of Giza in Egypt is about 137 metres high.

Reflection, rotation and translation

See Q1

How is a shape reflected?

A **reflection** flips the shape over to give a **mirror image**.

A reflection is the same distance as the shape from the **mirror line**.

The same shape reflected about different mirror lines

See Q2

How is a shape rotated?

A **rotation** turns the shape through an **angle**.

Rotations can be **clockwise** or **anticlockwise**.

The same shape rotated through different angles

90° anticlockwise

180° clockwise

See Q3

How is a shape translated?

A **translation** is a **sliding** movement.

Translations may be to the left or right, up or down, or a combination of these.

4 squares right

3 squares down

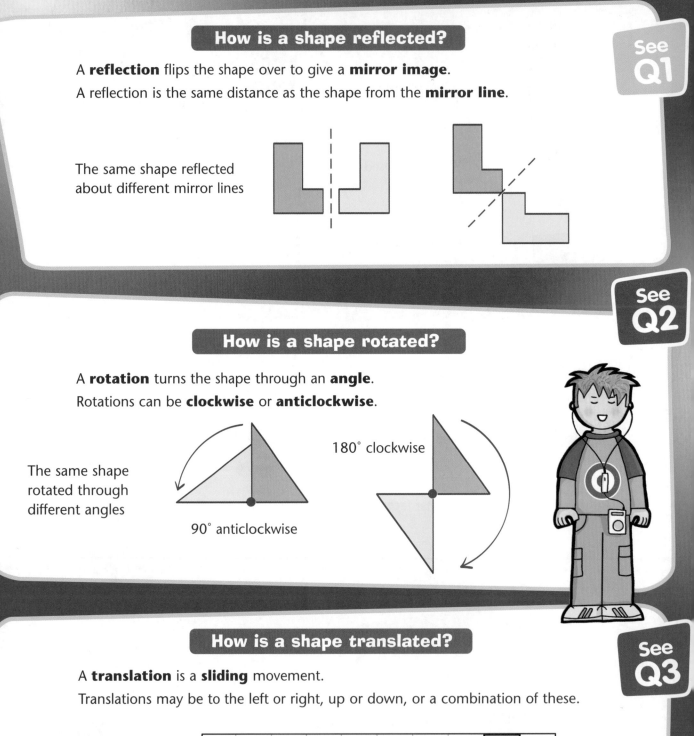

Reflect the shape in the mirror line to complete the face.

What did the angry shape do when it saw its reflection in the mirror?

It flipped!

Q2

A shape may be rotated through 90° (a right angle) three times to make a pattern. Rotate the green shape to complete the pattern.

Q3

Move the counter on the chessboard by following these instructions. Draw the position of the counter after each translation.

3 squares right
5 squares up
2 squares right
4 squares down

Did You Know?

A kaleidoscope works by reflecting tiny pieces of coloured glass in two or three long mirrors to make symmetrical patterns.

Quick Quiz

Use the following words to complete the sentences.

mirror   left   up   flips   down
right   turns

1   A rotation .... a shape.

2   A translation may move a shape sideways to

    the .... or ....

3   A translation may move a shape vertically

    .... or ....

4   A reflection .... a shape over.

5   A reflection gives a .... image.

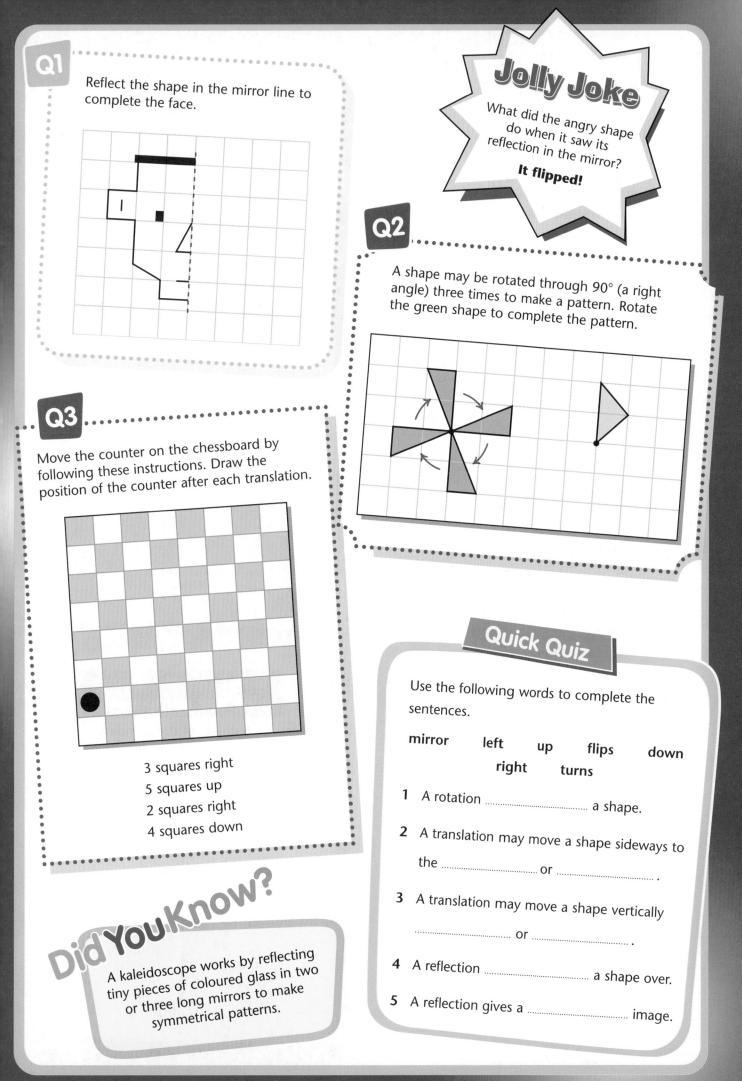

Position and coordinates

See Q1

How do I describe a position on a grid?

Coordinates are used to describe a point on a grid. To plot the point from its coordinates first go to the **right** then **up**.

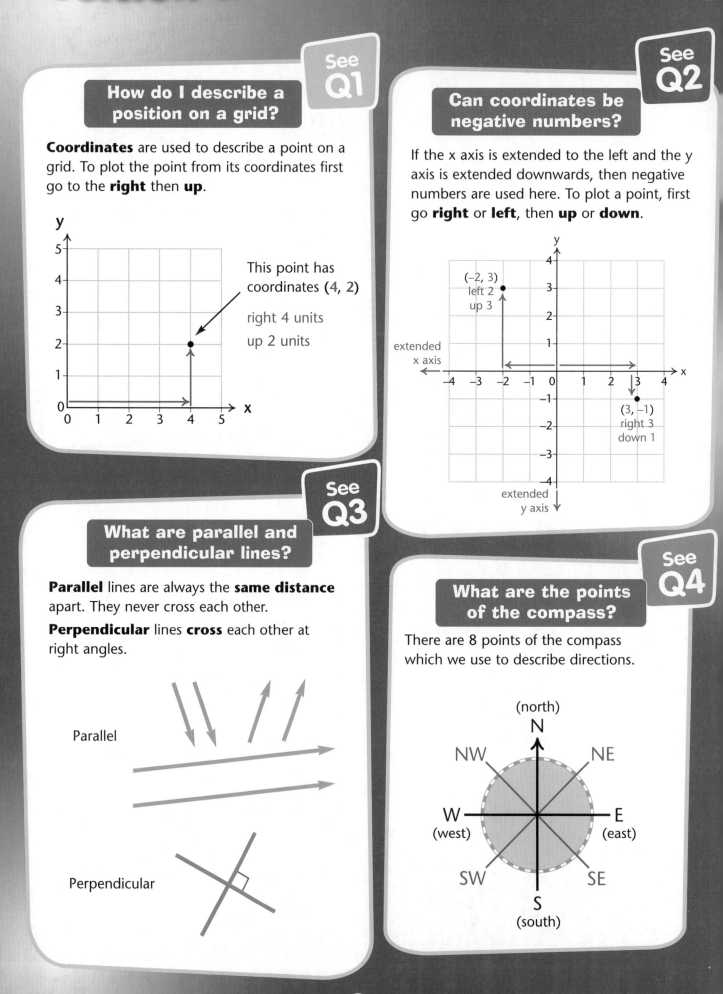

This point has coordinates (**4, 2**)

right 4 units

up 2 units

See Q2

Can coordinates be negative numbers?

If the x axis is extended to the left and the y axis is extended downwards, then negative numbers are used here. To plot a point, first go **right** or **left**, then **up** or **down**.

(−2, 3)
left 2
up 3

extended x axis

extended y axis

(3, −1)
right 3
down 1

See Q3

What are parallel and perpendicular lines?

Parallel lines are always the **same distance** apart. They never cross each other.

Perpendicular lines **cross** each other at right angles.

Parallel

Perpendicular

See Q4

What are the points of the compass?

There are 8 points of the compass which we use to describe directions.

(north)
N
NW
NE
W (west)
E (east)
SW
SE
S
(south)

Q1

Write down the coordinates of the points on this grid.

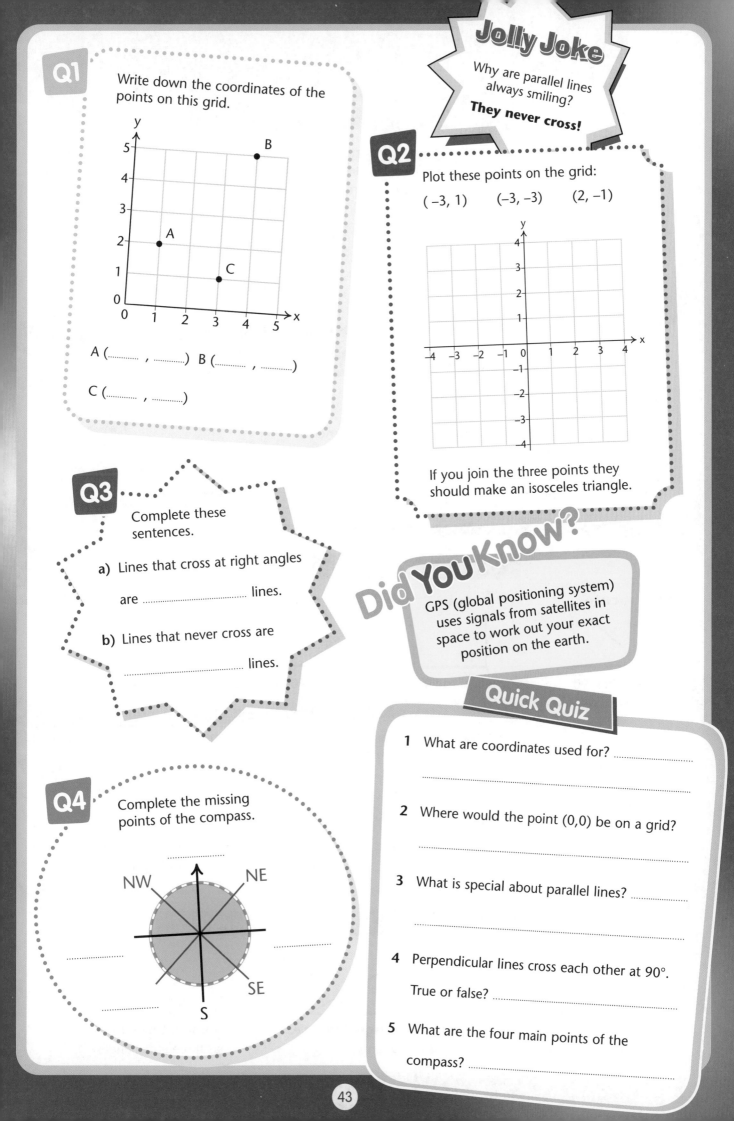

A (............ , ...) B (............ , ...)

C (............ , ...)

Q2

Plot these points on the grid:

(–3, 1)   (–3, –3)   (2, –1)

If you join the three points they should make an isosceles triangle.

Q3

Complete these sentences.

a) Lines that cross at right angles are .... lines.

b) Lines that never cross are .... lines.

Did You Know?

GPS (global positioning system) uses signals from satellites in space to work out your exact position on the earth.

Q4

Complete the missing points of the compass.

....

NW   NE

....

....   SE

S

Quick Quiz

1   What are coordinates used for? ....
....

2   Where would the point (0,0) be on a grid?
....

3   What is special about parallel lines? ....
....

4   Perpendicular lines cross each other at 90°.
   True or false? ....

5   What are the four main points of the compass? ....

43

Angles

See Q1

What is an angle?

An angle is a measure of turn. Angles are measured in **degrees** (°).

$\frac{1}{4}$ turn = 90° $\frac{1}{2}$ turn = 180° $\frac{3}{4}$ turn = 270°   1 full turn = 360°

See Q2

What do I use a protractor for?

A **protractor** is used to measure and draw angles.

110°

To measure: put the protractor cross over the corner of the angle, and read off the angle.

To draw: place the protractor cross on the end of your line, mark off the angle and join with a ruler.

See Q3

What types of angles are there?

acute   **right**   **obtuse**   **reflex**

less than 90°   equal to 90°   between 90° and 180°   greater than 180°

See Q4

What are 4 key facts about angles?

80°
140° 140°

110° 70°

45°

60°
60° 60°

angles at a **point** add up to 360°   angles on a **straight line** add up to 180° $\frac{1}{2}$ right angle is 45°   angles in a **triangle** add up to 180°

What do I need to know about triangles?

40°
70° 70°

60°
30°

60°
60° 60°

an **isosceles** triangle has two equal angles   a **right-angled** triangle has a 90° angle   an **equilateral** triangle has three equal angles

Q1

Fill in the missing blanks.

a) ....° = 1 full turn

b) 180° = ... turn

Q2

Using a protractor

a) Draw a 45° angle.

b) Measure this angle.

?

............°

Q3

Name these types of angle.

....

....

....

....

Q4

122°   ?

95°   48°

What is the angle of this slice of pizza?

............°

Quick Quiz

1 There are .... degrees in a right angle.

2 $\frac{3}{4}$ of a turn is equal to .... degrees.

3 Angles at a point add up to .... degrees.

4 An angle less than 90° is called an .... angle.

5 Angles in a triangle add up to .... degrees.

a) Work out the missing angle.

?
40°   30°   ....°

b) Without measuring the angles, which of these triangles is incorrect? Put a cross in it.

100°
45°   35°
70°
35°   75°

50°
40°   80°

45

Answers

Place value and ordering (page 3)

Q1 17204
Q2 **a)** 678 **b)** 5876 **c)** 19803
Q3 3.26 and 10.2; 12.67 and 2.39; 20.6 and 23.45
Q4 4.67, 5.46, 5.49, 6.52

Quick Quiz

1 8000
2 3489
3 4 tenths
4 Start with the largest
5 5.7

Rounding and estimating (page 5)

Q1 **a)** 2000 **b)** 5700
Q2 **a)** 5 **b)** 12 **c)** 11
Q3 4.67 and 4.7; 4.52 and 4.5; 4.58 and 4.6
Q4 £36 + £8 = £44

Quick Quiz

1 450
2 700
3 7000
4 35
5 2.6

Special numbers (page 7)

Q1 8732
Q2 **a)** 8 **b)** 30
Q3 15
Q4 **a)** Multiply a number by itself **b)** 4
Q5 **a)** –2 **b)** –3

Quick Quiz

1 Numbers that end in 1, 3, 5, 7 or 9
2 1, 2, 4, 8
3 9, 18, 27
4 16
5 Number that has only 2 factors, 1 and itself

Number sequences and patterns (page 9)

Q1 **a)** Add 5 **b)** 15
Q2 –4, –1
Q3 **a)** Multiply by 2 **b)** divide by 10 **c)** double then add 1
   d) multiply by 3
Q4

13 matchsticks are needed

Quick Quiz

1 A list of numbers that are linked by a rule
2 Add 3
3 20
4 –5
5 Double or multiply by 2

Fractions (page 11)

Q1 $\frac{5}{15}$
Q2 **a)** $\frac{1}{4}$ **b)** $\frac{1}{100}$ **c)** $\frac{1}{5}$
Q3 **a)** $\frac{2}{5}$ **b)** $\frac{2}{7}$ **c)** $\frac{3}{4}$
Q4 **a)** $1\frac{3}{5}$ **b)** $3\frac{1}{3}$
Q5 **a)** £4 **b)** £20

Quick Quiz

1 $\frac{9}{12}$
2 0.75
3 $\frac{5}{6}$
4 $\frac{2}{5}$
5 40

Percentages (page 13)

Q1 $\frac{3}{4}$ and 75%; $\frac{1}{10}$ and 10%; $\frac{1}{2}$ and 50%; $\frac{1}{100}$ and 1%
Q2 **a)**
Q3 **a)** £8 **b)** £16 **c)** £32
Q4 **a)** ✓ **b)** x **c)** ✓

Quick Quiz

1 75%
2 $\frac{1}{100}$
3 25%
4 7 kg
5 £6

Ratio and proportion (page 15)

Q1 **b)** There is 1 circle for every 4 squares
Q2 **b)**
Q3 400 g flour, 400 g butter, 400 g sugar, 8 eggs
Q4 6 girls

Quick Quiz

1 False
2 As a fraction
3 1 red for every 1 black
4 $\frac{2}{6}$ or $\frac{1}{3}$
5 $\frac{4}{6}$ or $\frac{2}{3}$

Addition and subtraction (page 17)

Q1 43 + 47 = 90; 67 + 18 = 85; 39 + 61 = 100; 23 + 32 + 27 = 82
Q2 **a)** ✓ **b)** x **c)** x
Q3 **a)** 1027 **b)** 4421

```
   3 7 8          1 9 7 0
 1 6 4 9 +      2 4 5 1 +
 1 0 2 7        4 4 2 1
```

Q4 **a)** 616 **b)** 1195

```
   8 4 3          2 5 6 9
   2 2 7 -        1 3 7 4 -
   6 1 6          1 1 9 5
```

Q5 **a)** 12.07 **b)** 4.68

```
   8. 6 7         7. 8 2
   3. 4 0 +       3. 1 4 -
 1 2. 0 7         4. 6 8
```

Quick Quiz

1 50
2 92
3 54
4 39
5 0.62

Multiplication and division (page 19)

Q1 6 x 8; 2 x 24; 16 x 3
Q2 **b)** 64 ÷ 8
Q3 **a)** 1792 **b)** 384

```
   2 5 6               2 4
       7 x            1 6 x
     4 2               2 4
   3 5 0             1 2 0
 1 4 0 0 +           2 4 0 +
 1 7 9 2             3 8 4
```

Q4 **a)** 27 r 3 **b)** 22

```
   1 6 5                 2 8 6
 - 1 6 2   27 x 6      - 1 3 0   10 x 13
       3      ↓          1 5 6   12 x 13
           27 r 3                  ↓
                                 2 2
```

Quick Quiz

1 64
2 144
3 9
4 7 r 2
5 280

Problem solving (page 21)

Q1 48 cards

46

Q2 **a)** 2100 m   **b)** 2.1 km
Q3 **a)** Casualty   **b)** Match of the Day
Q4 **a)** £3.15   **b)** £1.85   **c)** £4.80

Quick Quiz
1   80
2   1 hour 40 minutes
3   15p
4   1.35 m or 135 cm
5   £4.00

Probability (page 23)

Q1 **c)** It is certain that the month before May will be April
Q2 **b)**
Q3 $\frac{3}{7}$
Q4 Reading from left to right: 0, poor chance, even chance, good chance, certain

Quick Quiz
1   How likely it is that something happens
2   True
3   0 and 1
4   $\frac{1}{6}$
5   $\frac{1}{2}$

Mode, median, mean and range (page 25)

Q1 **a)** 3   **b)** 38
Q2 **a)** 39, 46, 48, 52, 56   **b)** 48
Q3 £7
Q4 **a)** Largest number minus smallest number   **b)** 11

Quick Quiz
1   Most common item or number
2   False
3   10
4   Median
5   5

Displaying data (page 27)

Q1 **a)** Numbers that are multiples of both 4 and 10
   b) 26 should be crossed out
Q2 **a)** Raffle   **b)** £700
Q3 **a)** 6 hours   **b)** 3 hours
Q4 **a)** 12 days   **b)** 10 days

Quick Quiz
1   Carroll diagram
2   Pie chart
3   Pictogram
4   Venn diagram
5   Bar chart

Units and measuring (page 29)

Q1 **a)** 1 m   **b)** 1000 g   **c)** 1000 ml   **d)** 100 cm
Q2 15 miles
Q3 **a)** 3 kg   **b)** 5.5 cm   **c)** 4000 m   **d)** 2500 ml
Q4 140 g

Quick Quiz
1   10 mm
2   2 pounds
3   2 litres
4   6000 m
5   2.4 litres

Perimeter and area (page 31)

Q1 23 cm
Q2 14 cm
Q3 Letter B should be coloured red
Q4
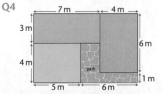

Quick Quiz
1   Perimeter
2   kg
3   Area
4   12 cm
5   Area = length x breadth

Time (page 33)

Q1

Q2 **a)** 24   **b)** 60
Q3

Q4 4 hours 10 minutes

Quick Quiz
1   30 days
2   120 minutes
3   21 days
4   3 minutes
5   14:30

2D shapes: triangles, quadrilaterals and polygons (page 35)

Q1 Tick **a)** and **c)**
Q2 Square ✓ ✓, parallelogram x x, rhombus ✓ x
Q3 False
Q4 **a)** Pentagon   **b)** octagon

Quick Quiz
1   Isosceles
2   It has one 90 degree angle
3   Trapezium
4   Square and rectangle
5   Hexagon

2D shapes: symmetry (page 37)

Q1
Q2
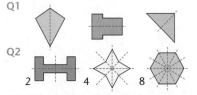
Q3 Tick second and fourth shapes

Quick Quiz
1   4
2   2
3   False
4   No
5   True

3D shapes (page 39)

Q1 Reading from top down: triangular prism, triangular-based pyramid, square-based pyramid
Q2 6 faces, 8 vertices; 4 vertices, 6 edges
Q3 **a)** Cylinder   **b)** sphere
Q4 Square-based pyramid

Quick Quiz
1   Cube
2   Vertex
3   Square
4   Sphere
5   Net

Reflection, rotation and translation (page 41)

Q1

Q2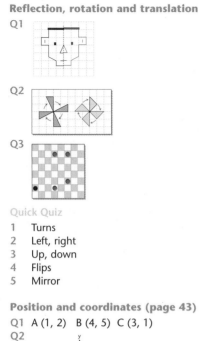

Q3

Quick Quiz

1   Turns
2   Left, right
3   Up, down
4   Flips
5   Mirror

Position and coordinates (page 43)

Q1   A (1, 2)   B (4, 5)   C (3, 1)

Q2

Q3   **a)** Perpendicular   **b)** parallel
Q4   Starting at top and reading clockwise: N, E, SW, W

Quick Quiz

1   To describe a point on a grid
2   Where the two axes cross
3   They are always the same distance apart
4   True
5   N, E, S, W

Angles (page 45)

Q1   **a)** 360°   **b)** $\frac{1}{2}$ turn

Q2   **a)**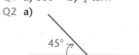

45°

b) 158°

Q3   Reflex, acute, obtuse, right

Q4   95°

Q5   **a)** 110°   **b)** the third triangle

50°

40°   80°

Quick Quiz

1   90 degrees
2   270 degrees
3   360 degrees
4   Acute
5   180 degrees